MANCHESTER
UNITED
THE BIGGEST AND THE BEST

Abbeville Press Publishers

New York · London

A portion of the book's proceeds are donated to the **Hugo Bustamante AYSO Playership Fund,** a national scholarship program to help ensure that no child misses the chance to play AYSO Soccer. Donations to the fund cover the cost of registration and a uniform for a child in need.

Text by Illugi Jökulsson

For the original edition
Design and layout: Ólafur Gunnar Guðlaugsson

For the English-language edition
Editor: Joan Strasbaugh
Production manager: Louise Kurtz
Designer: Ada Rodriguez
Copy editor: Ken Samuelson

PHOTOGRAPHY CREDITS

Getty Images
2–3 1968 European Championship final in Wembley: Popperfoto. 20–21 George Best: Bob Thomas. 26 Ferguson: Bob Thomas. 31 Eric Cantona and Peter Schmeichel: Getty. 38–39 Ole Gunnar Solskjaer: Ben Radford. P 46–47 Rooney: Alex Livesey. 48–49 Eiður and Keane: Matthew Peters.

Shutterstock
8, 9, 18, 19, 28, 29, 32, 33, 36, 37, 40, 41, 42, 43, 44, 45, 50, 51, 52, 53, 54, 55, 56, 57, 58, 59.

Please note: This book has not been authorized by **Manchester United** nor persons associated with it.

All statistics current through the 2012–2013 season unless otherwise noted.

First published in the United States of America in 2014 by Abbeville Press, 137 Varick Street, New York, NY 10013

First published in Iceland in 2012 by Sögur útgáfa, Fákafen 9, 108 Reykjavík, Iceland

First edition
10 9 8 7 6 5 4 3 2 1

Illugi Jvkulsson.
  [Manchester United. English]
  Manchester United : the biggest and the best / by Illugi Jvkulsson. — First edition.
      pages cm. — (World soccer legends)
  Translated from Icelandic.
  Summary: ""The history of Manchester United featuring stories about past and current stars, including Beckham, Giggs, Rooney, and others, as well as information on coaches Alex Ferguson and Matt Busby. Fun facts, stats, and a board game." — Provided by publisher.
  ISBN 978-0-7892-1162-0 (hardback)
  1. Manchester United (Soccer team)—History—Juvenile literature. I. Title.
    GV943.6.M3I5513 2014
    796.33409—dc23
                2013045802

For bulk and premium sales and for text adoption procedures, write to Customer Service Manager, Abbeville Press, 137 Varick Street, New York, NY 10013, or call 1-800-ARTBOOK.

Visit Abbeville Press online at www.abbeville.com.

CONTENTS

Manchester

Human settlement in the area of the City of Manchester began roughly 2,000 years ago. The Romans had conquered most of England around 80 AD, and they built a fortress on the highest point of a sandstone bluff that was said to resemble a woman's breast. The fortress was therefore named Mamucium, which is a Latinized Celtic word meaning "breast-shaped hill." The word for camp in Latin is castra and with time *Mamucium* and *castra* evolved into the name *Man-chester*. The peak disappeared a long time ago.

The Romans seem to have abandoned the settlement in the third or fourth century but civilian

The Romans ruled a large part of Europe from 200 BC to 400 AD. They founded Manchester.

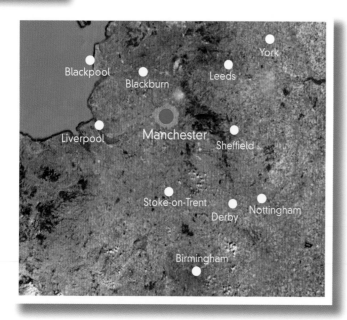

settlement continued in Manchester, even though it was only a small village for a long period of time. There was a crossing point close by over the River Irwell called Trafford. In the late 1700s Manchester started to expand rapidly, and Mancunians became known for their wool and cotton textiles. The Industrial

Largest Cities in the UK:

1. London	8 million
2. Birmingham	1 million
3. Leeds	770 thousand
4. Glasgow, Scotland	600 thousand
4. Sheffield	535 thousand
5. Manchester	505 thousand
6. Liverpool	440 thousand

There are smaller towns and boroughs around all English major cities that create large continuous urban areas. Around 2.2 million people live in the Greater Manchester Area.

Manchester just before 1900.

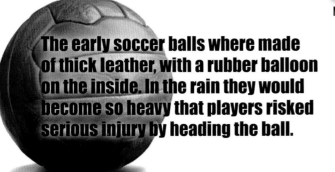

The early soccer balls where made of thick leather, with a rubber balloon on the inside. In the rain they would become so heavy that players risked serious injury by heading the ball.

The first soccer clubs in England were founded around 1860 in and near Sheffield. The first two clubs in Manchester were founded twenty years later.

Revolution led to a huge boom in the population of Manchester. Large factories were built to manufacture textiles and all sorts of machinery. Soon enough the city became one of the largest in England. In 1894 the Manchester Ship Canal, which ran 36 miles, was opened between Manchester and the port city of Liverpool. It was large enough for ocean-going ships to sail up river to Manchester. This explains why there is a ship in the crest of Manchester (and Manchester United) even though the city is inland.

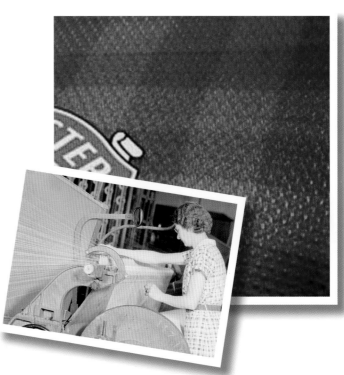

The design of Manchester United's controversial jersey for 2012–13 was inspired by the city's history in the textile industry.

Newton Heath's team in the early years of the club.

Newton Heath Becomes Manchester United

In 1878 the workers of the Lancashire and Yorkshire Railway depot at Newton Heath founded a soccer club they named for their place of work. The club first competed in the English Soccer League in 1892, and around that time it severed the ties to the railroad company and became an independent entity.

Unfortunately, Newton Heath soon ran into financial difficulties and in 1901 it was on the brink of bankruptcy. In order to raise funds, the club held a four-day bazaar that proved quite successful.

John Henry Davies

As legend has it, the team's captain Henry Stafford sent his St. Bernard dog around the crowd with a collection box around his neck. Unfortunately the dog wandered off and ended up on the doorstep of a local businessman called John Henry Davies. Davies had a daughter who immediately took to the dog so that when Stafford came looking, Davies offered to buy it from him. Stafford said that the girl could have the dog in return for a £500 investment from Davies in the club. Davies agreed and was appointed chairman and owner. The club was saved,

Manchester United 1904–1905

Clubs' Earlier Names

Arsenal	–	Dial Square
Liverpool	–	Everton Athletic
Tottenham	–	Hotspur F.C.
Everton	–	St. Domingo's
West Ham	–	Thames Ironworks F.C.
Newcastle	–	Newcastle East End F.C.
Manchester City	–	St. Mark's

Manchester City was founded in 1880. The club has always been a bitter rival of United. Manchester City has won three English championship titles. First in 1936–37, when United got relegated to the Second Division, and then in the seasons 1967–68 and 2011–12. United was the runner up on both occasions.

restructured and renamed Manchester United F.C. in 1902.

The fledgling club prospered under Davies' leadership. In 1907–08 the club won its first league title, and became FA Cup winner the following year. United reclaimed its first division title in 1910–11. By then the club had moved to new and superior grounds at Old Trafford.

In 1914 World War I broke out and the terrible war lasted until 1918. Young men in England were drafted to the war, and the English League was suspended for a several years.

After the Great War, the English Soccer League was revived. United struggled to get back on form, and for nearly 20 years it was an insignificant, middle-of-the-table club. The club even got relegated to the Second Division in 1922, where it remained for 3 years until it managed to establish itself again amongst the best clubs. Relegated again in 1931, United spent most of the thirties in the Second Division. In one season it nearly got relegated to the Third Division.

In 1938 United managed to get back into the First Division. Quite a few strong players had joined the club, and great efforts were put into building a stronger club. The soccer league was suspended again with the onslaught of World War II from 1939–45, but with the war over a new era began for United.

A St. Bernard dog had a big impact on United's history.

THE FIRST UNIFORMS

1878–1886

1887–1890

The Red Devils' Crest

United's crest is based on the City of Manchester's emblem. The ship in the city's emblem remains and shows Manchester as a city of trading and commerce, even though it was not a coastal port. For a long time there were stripes in both the city's and United's crest, but in 1970 United traded the stripes for the red devil. The devil refers to United's nickname "The Red Devils." The mastermind behind that change was United's manager, Matt Busby. See page 18.

Rooney

Giggs

In 1902, when Manchester United had changed its name, the club introduced a new uniform —the red shirt and white shorts. This has remained United's uniform ever since. Newton Heath (United's former name) played in completely different uniforms during its early years of existence and on this spread you can see how a few legendary United players would have looked in these different colors.

1893–1894   **1894–1896**   **1896–1902**

Evra   Scholes   Rio Ferdinand

A statue of Sir Busby outside Old Trafford Stadium.

BUSBY TURNED

From 1939–45 World War II raged in Europe, and England felt the full blow of it. The Soccer League was suspended and didn't start again until 1946–47. By then significant changes had been made at Manchester United, and a new manager, Matt Busby, had been appointed. He was young and energetic, and when he was hired he insisted on being given more administrative power in the club than was customary for managers to have at the time. Up until then most dealings regarding transfers, team selection and training had been in the hands of the club's board. Busby changed that and showed that he had more wits about him than most. With his managerial style the team played attacking soccer and scored a lot of goals. Manchester United immediately became one of the top clubs in the league under Busby, and in the 1951–52 season, the club became First Division champions for the first time in 41 years. The scorer Jack

Busby was a skilled soccer player before he became a manager. Remarkably, he only played for two clubs in his career and both of them were United's biggest rivals, first for Manchester City and then Liverpool. He was offered the position of assistant manager at Liverpool but the club wouldn't grant him the administrative powers he wanted and lost him to Manchester United.

SIR MATT BUSBY

UNITED INTO AN EMPIRE

Rowley flourished with United during this period.

United claimed the title again in 1955–56 and 1956–57, consequently establishing the club among the best clubs in Europe. For instance, United played against Real Madrid in the European Cup semifinals in 1957 and lost narrowly. Real Madrid was the greatest powerhouse of European soccer at the time.

Busby's boldness in using and trusting his youngest players produced a few raised eyebrows. Most of these youngsters were barely past twenty, and were therefore often called "the Busby Babes." Despite their young age they played like a well-oiled machine with their eyes fixed on the goal. And that goal was to win the European Cup in 1957–58 and dethrone Real Madrid.

THE BEST OF THE BUSBY BABES

There were many marvelous players among "the Busby Babes" but none so brilliant as Duncan Edwards. He was born in 1936 and made his debut for United in the First Division at the young age of 16, making him the youngest player to play in the top division. He usually played as a defensive midfielder but could easily operate in any position on the field. On one occasion he began as a striker and finished the game on defense. One of his fellow "Busby Babes," Bobby Charlton,

said: "Physically, he was enormous. He was strong and had a fantastic soccer brain. His ability was complete—right foot, left foot, long passing, short passing. He did everything instinctively."

Edwards was also very young when he was selected for the English national team and was widely considered to be a future captain for both United and England. Those who saw him play proclaim that he had the qualities to become one of the best players in history, on par with Pelé and Maradona. But sadly that was not to be.

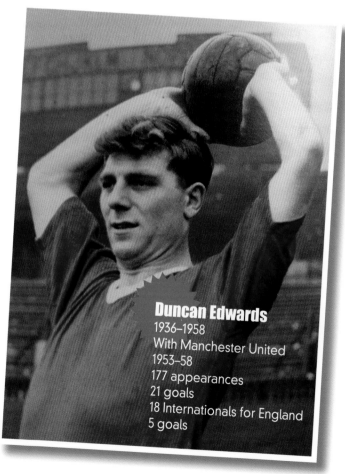

Duncan Edwards
1936–1958
With Manchester United
1953–58
177 appearances
21 goals
18 Internationals for England
5 goals

TRAGEDY

On February 6, 1958, a plane chartered by Manchester United was ready for takeoff at an airport in Munich, Germany, where it had refuelled. The team was on its way home from a European Cup match against Red Star Belgrade in Yugoslavia (now Serbia), and was through to the semifinals. The team was eager to get back to England in time to prepare for an important match against Wolves in the English First Division. United had a chance of winning for the third consecutive time. It had started to snow when the plane headed down the runway. A lot of slush had accumulated on the runway slowing the plane down so it didn't reach enough velocity to take off and crashed through a fence and into a house. Of the 44 people on board, 23 died. Among those who perished were eight members of United's team, including the team captain Roger Byrne. One of the players, the phenomenal Duncan Edwards, battled for his life for 15 days before dying in hospital. Many others were badly injured, such as the manager Busby who spent two months in hospital.

Goalkeeper Harry Gregg displayed great courage, refusing to leave the scene before he had managed to save as many of his teammates as he could from the wreck, and also a pregnant Yugoslavian lady and her young daughter.

This was of course a great blow to United and the city of Manchester. The club showed a lot of grit and continued to compete, but it took several years to recover and regain their previous form.

PLAYERS WHO PERISHED

 Roger Byrne, age 28, fullback, 245 appearances, 17 goals

 Duncan Edwards, age 21, midfielder, 151 appearances, 20 goals

 Tommy Taylor, age 26, striker, 166 appearances, 112 goals

 Eddie Colman, age 21, defender, 85 appearances, 1 goal

 David Pegg, age 22, winger, 127 appearances, 24 goals

 Liam "Billy" Whelan, age 22, winger, 79 appearances, 43 goals

 Mark Jones, age 24, center back, 103 appearances, 1 goal

 Geoff Bent, age 25, fullback, 12 appearances, 0 goals

IN MUNICH

Two of the survivors, John Berry and Jackie Blanchflower, were so severely injured in the crash that they never played soccer again. They had both been regulars on the team, and it was later revealed that the club didn't offer them the support they deserved after the crash.

OTHER FATALITIES
Two crew members
Three of the Manchester United staff
Eight journalists
Two other passengers

Harry Gregg was United's goalkeeper from 1957 to 1966. Some believe he was the club's best goalkeeper of all time, but as luck would have it, he never won any medals with the club due to unfortunate injuries at key moments in his career. Just a few months after the Munich tragedy he was chosen the best goalkeeper of the World Cup in Sweden in 1958, where he played for Northern Ireland.

THE RED DEVILS

Manchester United took a long time to recover after the tragedy in Munich, and did not win a title for several years. Slowly but surely Matt Busby started to build a new champion team. He now wanted to put aside all talk of the "Busby Babes," no longer finding the nickname appropriate as many of the players referred to had died in the air disaster, and also because he felt it was too juvenile and not likely to frighten opponents. So he decided to find a new moniker. He remembered a neighboring English rugby team, the Salford City Reds, that toured France in 1934. The team had worn red shirts and played rough and hard, prompting the French press to call them "les diables rouges" or "the Red Devils." Busby decided to adopt the name to intimidate opposing teams and to suggest that his players where a force to be reckoned with. In 1970 United added a devil to its crest.

In 1963 United won the FA Cup for the third time. In the season of 1964–65 the team then claimed the league title for the 6th time after going 8 years without winning it. United was crowned champion again a couple of years later and were clearly one of the major clubs in England, and in fact in all of Europe.

There were many fantastic players on the mighty '70s team, but three of the Red Devils are true legends. In 2008 a statue of the trio was erected at Old Trafford. Here they are from left to right: George Best, Denis Law, and Bobby Charlton. They were all crowned European Soccer Player of the Year—first Denis Law in 1964, then Charlton in 1966, and finally Best in 1968.

THE UNITED TRINITY
BEST LAW CHARLTON

Bobby Charlton was one of the original "Busby Babes," and one of the people saved by Harry Gregg from the plane wreckage in Munich. He recovered quickly and remained one of the key players in Busby's squad. Charlton was regarded as an extremely intelligent and graceful player. He began his career as a striker, but had a big impact on developing a new role on the field of the attacking midfielder. He was an outstanding player with both United and the English national team.

Bobby Charlton
England
Born 1937
With United 1956–73
758 appearances
249 goals
106 Internationals for England
49 goals

Before taking off in Munich in 1958 the United player Tommy Taylor switched seats with Bobby Charlton. He thought Charlton's original seat was safer than his, in case of accident. This almost certainly saved Charlton's life, as Taylor was killed in the crash, together with those sitting next to him.

Denis Law transferred to United from Torino in Italy, but had previously played for Huddersfield and Manchester City. He was a superb scorer and made goals of every variety. He still holds many records for United—no one has, for example, scored as many goals in one season, or a total of 46 goals in 1963–64. No other player has scored as many hat tricks, 18 in all. Unfortunately, Law

Denis Law
Scotland
Born 1940
With United 1962–73
404 appearances
237 goals
55 Internationals for Scotland
30 goals

was injured before the European Cup final in 1968 and missed the match, but he played a big part in turning United into one of the strongest teams in Europe.

Denis Law's family was so poor that he didn't get soccer boots until a neighbor gave him a pair for his 16th birthday.

England became World Champion in 1966 when the World Cup was hosted in England. The home team defeated West Germany 4–2 in extra time. Two United players took part in the game. Bobby Charlton steered the attack from midfield, and Nobby Stiles as a defensive midfielder did his utmost to break down the opponents' attacks. He played very well but became especially famous for taking out his dentures after the final, dancing around the field with the World Cup in one hand and his dentures in the other. He was never shy about his missing front teeth.

Nobby Stiles

Although Manchester United is known for its attacking soccer, the defense has never been neglected. One of United's best defenders of all time was Bill Foulkes, who was with the club for 18 seasons from 1951–70. He was born in 1932, played a total of 688 games for United and scored 9 goals. Foulkes survived the plane crash in Munich and he and Harry Gregg helped people out of the wreck. He felt he didn't fully get over the incident until he got to lift the European Cup in 1968.

Billy Foulkes

SIMPLY THE BEST

George Best
Northern Ireland
1946–2005
With United 1963–74
474 appearances
181 goals
Internationals for Northern Ireland
37 appearances
9 goals

Best taking no prisoners.

Like every major club, United employs scouts who keep an eye out for promising soccer players all over the world. In 1961 one of United's scouts in Northern Ireland sent a telegram to the club's manager, Matt Busby, saying: "I think I've found you a genius."

He was not exaggerating. Here was a boy at the age of 15 who was so small and light that his local club had rejected him. But the scout spotted how gifted he was and was confident that this boy could go very far. Busby was curious, and in 1963 George Best made his debut for United at the tender age of 17. And soon enough he proved that he truly was a genius. He was unbelievably tricky with the ball and had the great ability to throw off defenders and goalkeepers. He could play in several positions, but most often as an attacking left winger. Many of his numerous goals were absolutely phenomenal.

Best was extremely popular, which was no surprise because on top of his stellar soccering talents, he was cheerful, outgoing, and good looking. His extravagant lifestyle and love life often provided sensational headlines, and he was the first real celebrity soccer player, frequently gracing the gossip pages of the papers, not just the sport sections. Subsequently his lifestyle took its toll. Seriously afflicted by alcoholism, Best saw his health and career start to deteriorate well before his thirtieth birthday. He left United in 1974 and died in 2005.

Best once scored 6 goals in one game. That was in a Cup match in February 1970 against Northampton that played in Fourth Division. United won 8–2.

Ten years after the tragedy at Munich, United fulfilled the fans' long-awaited dream of winning the European Cup. In the qualifiers, United showed great strength and knocked Real Madrid out in the semifinals. George Best scored the winning goal in the first match at Old Trafford.

The final was held at Wembley Stadium in London on May 29 against Benfica from Portugal, which was one of the biggest clubs of European soccer at the time, with the fabulous Eusébio leading the attack. Just before the final whistle of normal time, Benfica seemed about to snatch a winner as Eusébio broke through United's defense alone. But United's goalkeeper, Alex Stepney, made a such a crucial and dramatic save that even Eusébio himself applauded.

United dominated the match in extra time. George Best got the ball 25 yards from the goal, dashed into the penalty area by swerving past the Benfica defense, and then dribbled round the onrushing goalkeeper and rolled the ball into the abandoned goal. Brian Kidd added United's third goal with a powerful header. Five minutes later the great Bobby Charlton appropriately scored his second goal of the game.

United was finally acknowledged as the best soccer club in Europe. No one was happier than Matt Busby. A dream that seemed to have perished in Munich had finally been realized.

Brian Kidd scoring United's third goal. It was his 19th birthday. Kidd would stay with United until 1974. Also celebrating is the Man of the Match, John Aston.

MPIONS AT LAST!

The Red Devils wore their dark blue away uniform when they won that monumental victory.

1

EUROPEAN CUP

May 29, 1968
Wembley Stadium, London, England

MAN.UNITED — BENFICA

4–1

Charlton 53, 99	Graça 75
Best 93	
Kidd 94	

After extra time

Stepney
Brennan – Foulkes – Sadler – Dunne
Crerand – Bobby Charlton – Stiles
George Best – Brian Kidd Aston

23

UNITED RELEGATED!

Law scoring the famous goal.

There are many intense moments in United's history. Few were as dramatic as the "Denis Law Moment" on April 27, 1974.

Law was one of United's greatest scorers of all time, but after 11 years he was given a free transfer and joined Manchester City. He was still friends with his old teammates at United and held in high esteem at Old Trafford. United had been doing abysmally the season in question and when City and United met, the latter needed a win to avoid being relegated, which would of course be a serious blow to the club and its supporters. The match was rough and tough, and on the 81st minute the ball found Law in the box, and he scored with a smooth heel kick. The goal was a product of a great striker's instinct, but Law was taken aback. He, and everybody else, believed he had just consigned his former team to the dark abyss of the Second Division! So Law didn't celebrate the goal and City's manager substituted him immediately to save him from the screaming mob, some of which charged onto the field. Law walked off with his head down. He did, however, have the courage to go to the pub later in the evening, where members of both United and City sat down for a pow-wow pint. In an interview with *Mail Online* in 2011, Law said he still felt a bit bad over the goal.

As it turned out, results of other matches in the league lined up so that the outcome of the United-City game didn't matter—United would have been relegated anyway.

To the credit of United supporters, they were quick to forgive their old idol, who had served them so well for so long.

Dry Spell

After phenomenal success in the sixties, United had started a downhill struggle. Matt Busby was starting to tire and retired as manager in 1969, though he returned a year later to manage the team for one more season. But by then he and his team were

Law and Busby

spent. There was a lack of new talent to fill their shoes, and United declined surprisingly rapidly. After a few mediocre seasons the unthinkable happened: Manchester United, the European Champions of 1968, were relegated in 1974.

Though the club's fall from glory only lasted one season, and it was back in the top league a year later, United didn't seem to be able to regain its former status. The club did manage the occasional success, winning the FA Cup three times over the next decade—first against Liverpool in 1977, then beating Brighton in 1983, and finally Everton in 1985.

A NEW BUSBY NEEDED!
But the First Division League title continued to evade United, and so the club didn't make it to the European Cup either. At the same time, the club's archrival, Liverpool, was on a roll, winning numerous trophies both in England and in Europe.

In the season of 1985–1986 change seemed to be in the air. Their colorful and charismatic manager, Ron Atkinson, led the team to ten victories in the first ten rounds of the first league. The multi-talented midfield maestro and team captain Bryan Robson was in his very best form. But after the holidays Manchester United hit a slump and ended in fourth place, while Liverpool claimed the trophy yet again.

The club was off to a bad start the following season and in November 1986 Manchester United was in danger of being relegated again. The owners were not ready to accept that outcome and fired Atkinson. The club needed a new Busby who could restore the club to its former glory.

Bryan Robson was one of United's most brilliant players of all time, though the club certainly had its ups and downs in his time. He delighted soccer fans with his fighting spirit, vision, and skill. He was captain of United for 12 years (1982–94), longer than any other captain in the club's history. And it was fitting that he should end his career by scoring the decisive goal in the season's final game when United finally won the Premier League in 1992–93. In 2011 former and current United players elected Robson as the best player in United's history, ahead of George Best, Bobby Charlton, Paul Scholes, Ryan Giggs, and Roy Keane.

Bryan Robson
Born in 1957
With United 1981–94
461 appearances
99 goals
90 Internationals for England
26 goals

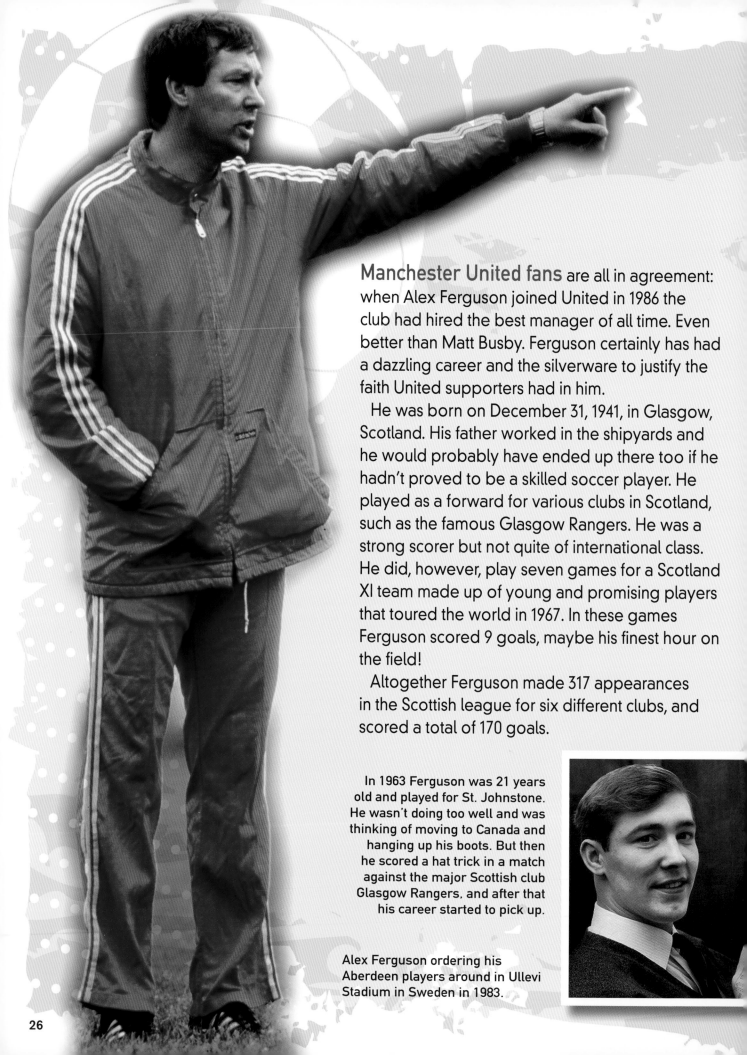

Manchester United fans are all in agreement: when Alex Ferguson joined United in 1986 the club had hired the best manager of all time. Even better than Matt Busby. Ferguson certainly has had a dazzling career and the silverware to justify the faith United supporters had in him.

He was born on December 31, 1941, in Glasgow, Scotland. His father worked in the shipyards and he would probably have ended up there too if he hadn't proved to be a skilled soccer player. He played as a forward for various clubs in Scotland, such as the famous Glasgow Rangers. He was a strong scorer but not quite of international class. He did, however, play seven games for a Scotland XI team made up of young and promising players that toured the world in 1967. In these games Ferguson scored 9 goals, maybe his finest hour on the field!

Altogether Ferguson made 317 appearances in the Scottish league for six different clubs, and scored a total of 170 goals.

In 1963 Ferguson was 21 years old and played for St. Johnstone. He wasn't doing too well and was thinking of moving to Canada and hanging up his boots. But then he scored a hat trick in a match against the major Scottish club Glasgow Rangers, and after that his career started to pick up.

Alex Ferguson ordering his Aberdeen players around in Ullevi Stadium in Sweden in 1983.

THE SAVIOR

Ferguson is known for his sharp wit and irony. He once said of Kenny Dalglish, a fellow Scotsman, rival and good friend: "Kenny only has a few true friends, but there's nothing wrong with that, because at the end of the day, you only need six people to carry your coffin."

Ferguson had a temper on him when he was younger, and can still get quite testy. When he was manager of Aberdeen he once fined one of his players, John Hewitt, for overtaking his car on a public road.

In 1974 he hung up his boots and became a manager for St. Mirren in Scotland. He worked miracles for the team but was fired four years later for alleged breach of contract despite his success. He was then hired by Aberdeen, which is one of Scotland's stronger clubs.

The two Glasgow clubs, Rangers and Celtic, have towered over the soccer scene in Scotland, and other clubs hardly ever win the league. Yet during Ferguson's eight-year stint as manager of Aberdeen, the club won the title three times. That truly was an incredible feat. In addition, Aberdeen won the Scottish Cup four times, and the Scottish League Cup once. In the season of 1982–83 Aberdeen exceeded all expectations and won the European Cup

Winners' Cup. In the quarterfinals Ferguson's players beat the German giants Bayern Munich. Aberdeen made it to the final in Ullevi Stadium in Sweden, like David against Goliath—the Spanish giant of Real Madrid. Aberdeen beat the Spaniards 2–1 in extra time. It was a mammoth achievement for Aberdeen and Ferguson. The Swedish audience watching the young manager celebrate in Ullevi Stadium could not have imagined the incredible career that lay ahead of this young Scotsman.

Ferguson found it was time to move to bigger things. He was invited to manage the Rangers, and English clubs like the Wolves, Tottenham, and Arsenal. Liverpool allegedly even considered hiring him. But Ferguson turned every offer down until November 1986. Manchester United had been struggling to get back to form. The club had started the season badly and was at risk of being relegated. Ron Atkinson was fired and Ferguson was asked to take his place. Ferguson accepted the challenge, full of hope and confidence, but even he could not have imagined what lay in store.

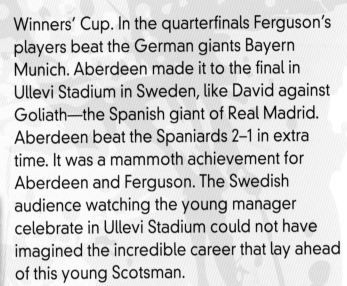

His full name is Alexander Chapman Ferguson. His wife is named Cathy. They got married in 1966 and have three sons—Mark (born in 1968), and the twins Darren and Jason (born in 1972). Darren became a soccer player and played for United under his father's management, but never made it to the top.

THE FIRST TITLES!

It was not an easy task for Alex Ferguson to install discipline and ambition in United, in order to pull the club out of the slump and back to the top of the league. The first seasons were not without incident and towards the end of 1989 there were rumors that Ferguson would soon be sacked because of the club's poor performance. These rumors were unfounded, United's management was confident it had the right man to rebuild the club.

That trust would pay off. In May 1990 United won their first trophy under Ferguson's leadership when the club beat Crystal Palace in the FA Cup final. The following year, United showed that they were on par with Europe's best clubs by beating Barcelona's "Dream Team" in the UEFA Cup Winners' Cup. And in 1992 United won the League Cup.

But it was not until the following season, 1992–93, that the holy grail, the English championship, was finally in sight. By now the Premier League had been established and the dominating club of the past 15 years, Liverpool, was losing momentum. Arsenal and Leeds were also in decline, and teams like Norwich and Aston Villa topped the standings for most of the season. Ferguson had focused on building a disciplined, attacking soccer team that was perfected with the purchase of the French striker Eric Cantona. At the end of the season United claimed the Premier League title, with a 10-point margin over the runners-up, Aston Villa. Norwich City came third.

The 26-year wait was over for Manchester United fans.

FERGIE'S FLEDGLINGS

Even the most hopeful, enthusiastic United supporters could not have imagined the incredible run that was to begin in 1993. Many would have expected the club to fall back into decline when the strong players who brought the title back to Old Trafford started to age—players like the powerful defenders Steve Bruce, Denis Irwin, and Gary Pallister, midfielders Brian McClair and Paul Ince, and forward, Hughes. But that was not to be. Ferguson's foresight and vision became clear in the following seasons. He put a herculean effort into rebuilding the team and over the next years he introduced several very young players to the team, called Fergie's Fledglings, who proved to be even stronger and better trained than the "Busby Babes" had been. They included players like Paul Scholes, Nicky Butt, Gary and Phil Neville, David Beckham, and last but not least, Ryan Giggs. When they joined United's first team one by one in the late 1990s, the club became stronger than it had ever been.

The Premier League Championship Team 1992–93

Peter Schmeichel
Steve Bruce Gary Pallister
Paul Parker   Denis Irwin
Paul Ince Lee Sharpe
Brian McClair   Ryan Giggs
Mark Hughes Eric Cantona

The Russian winger Andrei Kanchelskis also played a great deal during this season, as did the multi-talented Clayton Blackmore and Ferguson's son, Darren. The top scorers were Hughes with 16 goals, Giggs with 11, and McClair and Cantona with 9 each.

SCHOLES

Paul Scholes, along with Ryan Giggs, was the epitome of the qualities that characterized United's championship teams. He was a box-to-box midfielder who never gave up and scored a multitude of goals. He was capable of some brutal tackles in his career, but weighing against that is, for example, this sentiment from the Spanish genius Xavi: "He's a role model. In the last 15 to 20 years the best central midfielder that I have seen—the most complete—is Scholes. He's a spectacular player who has everything. He can play the final pass, he can score, he is strong, he never gets knocked off the ball, and he doesn't give possession away."

Paul Scholes
Born in 1974
Debuted in 1993
718 appearances
155 goals
66 Internationals for England
14 goals

Scholes has a fiery temperament and can sometimes lose his sense of judgement. No other player has been booked as often in the UEFA Champions League.

Scholes announced his retirement in 2011 at the age of 36. When United lost several key players due to injuries later in the season, Scholes knocked on Ferguson's door offering to come out of retirement. Ferguson took him up on the offer and Scholes showed that he had by no means lost his touch. He then retired for good in 2013.

CANTONA AND SCHMEICHEL

The beginning of Manchester United's glory days in the last decade of the 20th century will always be associated with two fiery soccer players.

CANTONA

In 1992 the French striker was lured to United from Leeds, where he had been playing for a season. He was known in his native France for his fighting spirit, scoring abilities, and extremely fiery temperament. He had an instant impact on Manchester United—he oozed confidence and it rubbed off, and definitely played a part in delivering United the first Premiership title.

Cantona was a unique character and became so crucial to the team that Alex Ferguson was willing to turn a blind eye to his occasionally erratic behavior. But on January 25, 1995, he went too far. He was sent off in a match against Crystal Palace and on his way to the tunnel he turned and kung-fu kicked a mocking Palace supporter and then punched him several times. He was sentenced to community service and an eight-month ban. Most people thought his career was over.

After Cantona retired from soccer he appeared in several movies, often playing a tough guy.

But "King Eric" returned and continued to score spectacular goals for United. He had learned to better control his temper, and Ferguson made him captain in 1996–97. Cantona retired at the age of thirty and later said: "I loved the game, but I no longer had the passion to go to bed early, not to go out with my friends . . . and do the things I like in life."

SCHMEICHEL

Alex Ferguson bought the great Dane in 1991 and Schmeichel's tremendous goalkeeping skills played a huge part in United's success. Schmeichel was big and confident, but also incredibly agile. His teammates could always count on him to keep the goal safe. Schmeichel became European Champion with the Denmark national team in 1992. After leaving United he played for three other clubs, including Manchester City for one season.

Schmeichel is half Polish, and his middle name is Boleslaw.

Eric Cantona
Born in 1966
With United 1992–97
185 appearances
82 goals
45 Internationals for
France
20 goals

Peter Schmeichel
Born in 1963
393 appearances
1 goal
129 Internationals for
Denmark
1 goal

"THEATER

Bobby Charlton was the first to refer to Old Trafford as the "Theater of Dreams." The home grounds of Manchester United were inaugurated in 1910, and it has gone through several renovations and refurbishments since then. It is the dream of many soccer players all over the world to play on this field. The plan is to enlarge the spectator area by 15,000 seats so that the stadium will eventually have a capacity of 90,000 people.

During WWII Old Trafford was used as a military depot. This resulted in a German air-strike on the stadium that caused considerable damage.

OF DREAMS"

The largest soccer stadiums in the UK

1.	Wembley Stadium, London	90,000
2.	Old Trafford, Manchester	75,900
3.	Celtic Park, Glasgow	60,800
4.	Emirates Stadium, London	60,300
5.	St. James' Park, Newcastle	52,400
6.	Ibrox Stadium, Glasgow	51,100
7.	Stadium of Light, Sunderland	49,000
8.	Etihad Stadium, Manchester	47,800
9.	Anfield, Liverpool	45,300
10.	Villa Park, Birmingham	42,800

Europe's largest:

Camp Nou, Barcelona	98,800
Santiago Bernabéu, Madrid	85,500
Stade de France, París	81,300
San Siro, Milan	80,000

Fergie's Biggest Mistake

Jaap Stam became the most expensive defender in soccer history when United bought him from PSV Eindhoven for 10.6 million pounds in 1998. The big, strong Dutchman immediately became a regular rock in United's defense. Some people consider him United's strongest defender ever. Three years later, due to various misunderstandings and a rare error of judgment, Alex Ferguson sold Stam to Lazio. He continued to play at the highest level for six years and Ferguson later admitted that selling Stam had probably been his greatest mistake while he was boss at Old Trafford.

FOREIGN PLAYERS AT OLD TRAFFORD

Nowadays soccer is truly international and the strongest teams in the world, like United, search for players all over the globe. But this hasn't always been the case. For the first 90 years of United's history, foreign players didn't appear at all for United—that is, if we exclude Scottish, Welsh, and Irish players. Also excluded are a few players from Canada or the USA who can really be considered British. (See page 53.)

The first ten truly foreign players to play at Old Trafford were:

1. Carlo Sartori, Italy		1968
2. Nikola Jovanovic, Yugoslavia		1980
3. Arnold Mühren, Holland		1982
4. Jesper Olsen, Denmark		1984
5. John Sivebæk, Denmark		1986
6. Mark Bosnich, Australia		1990
7. Andrei Kanchelskis, Ukraine		1991
8. Peter Schmeichel, Denmark		1991
9. Eric Cantona, France		1992
10. William Prunier, France		1995

Carlo Sartori didn't look particularly Italian with his bright red hair, and in fact he grew up in Manchester. But he was born in Italy in 1948 of Italian parents who moved to England when the boy was only a few years old. He emerged through the ranks of United and in October 1968 came on as a substitute in a league game against Tottenham on White Hart Lane.

Sartori was a decent midfielder but never quite broke into the main team. In five years he played 55 games, scoring six goals. In 1973 he left and played for a number of years for Bologna and other Italian teams. When he retired, he returned to Manchester and worked in his father's successful company as a professional knife-sharpener for hotels and restaurants, eventually taking over the business.

Nikola Jovanovic was a highly regarded Yugoslavian international defender who signed with United in 1980. United paid Red Star of Belgrade 300,000 pounds for his services, making him one of the club's most expensive players at the time! Unfortunately, Jovanovic didn't make the grade at Old Trafford and he left having played only 21 league games. He did, however, manage to score 4 goals.

Arnold Mühren was already a respected attacking midfielder when he arrived at Old Trafford in 1982, having played for Ajax and Twente in his native Holland and then for a very strong Ipswich team. Mühren became quite a success with United during his three year stay. He played 70 league games, scoring 13 goals. He then returned to Ajax and was an intregral part of the elegant Dutch team that won the European Championship in 1987.

Giggs' grandfather is from Sierra Leone

Ryan Giggs
Ryan Giggs
Born in 1973
Debuted 1991
941 appearances
168 goals
64 Internationals
for Wales
12 goals

BARCLAYS

THE LEGENDARY GIGGS

Ryan Giggs was born on November 29, 1973, in Cardiff, Wales. His family moved from Wales when Ryan was six years old. His father was a rugby player and was signed by a club in the Manchester area. The youngster quickly demonstrated great soccer intelligence and United's manager, Alex Ferguson, did not waste any time when he saw him play at the age of 13. He got Giggs to sign with United and his career skyrocketed. He debuted with United on March 2, 1991, when he came on as a substitute in a league game against Everton. United lost the match but the 17-year-old Giggs had begun his amazingly long and successful career. Through most of his career he played as a left winger, but recently he has played in central midfield.

In August 2013, Giggs began his 24th season with United. At the time he had played an amazing 941 games and scored 168 goals. Many of his goals were extremely important but his principal gifts are amazing vision, pinpoint passes, and a fine blend of agility and pace. Giggs has become a United legend. Many great soccer players have played for United, but none have served the club for as long as he has with such commitment and enthusiasm.

One of Giggs' greatest goals was in the FA Cup semifinals against Arsenal on April 14, 1999. He got the ball almost in the middle of his own half, raced up the field, swerving past four defenders who tried to catch him, and finally blasted the ball into the top of the net past Arsenal's goalkeeper, David Seaman. Take a look on YouTube!

"Only two players made me cry when watching soccer, one was Diego Maradona, the other was Ryan Giggs."

THE INCREDIBLE VICTORY OVER BAYERN MUNICH

Manchester United won an incredible victory in the 1999 UEFA Champions League Final. The club was up against Bayern Munich and the Germans took the lead early on, when Mario Basler scored from a free kick in the 6th minute. United struggled with creating dangerous chances and when the normal 90 minutes were up the Germans were already celebrating. As the official indicated three minutes of injury time, United won a corner and Peter Schmeichel joined the attack in the Bayern penalty area.

Solskjaer celebrates his famous goal. Bayern's Oliver Kahn and Marcus Babbel watch in astonishment.

After a short scuffle in the penalty area the ball landed at the feet of Teddy Sheringham who swiped the ball into the net, scoring the equalizer. United seemed to have forced extra time, but then the team won another corner. Beckham swung the corner again, Sheringham headed the ball down towards Ole Gunnar Solskjær who kicked the ball into the roof of the goal. Manchester United was European Champion once again after this.

2

UEFA Champions League

May 26, 1999
Camp Nou, Barcelona, Spain

MAN. UNITED–BAYERN MUNICH

2–1

Sheringham 92   Basler 8
Solskjaer 94

Schmeichel
Gary Neville – Johnsen – Stam – Irwin
Blomqvist (Sheringham 67) – Butt – Beckham – Giggs
Yorke – Cole (Solskjaer 81)

THE 21ST-CENTURY CHAMPIONS

Manchester United's victorious run has continued to the present day. Arsenal was the club's most dangerous rival for a while, and later Chelsea and then neighbors Manchester City, but United has always come back as a winner. Sir Alex Ferguson always had a knack for finding and training young, spectacular talents. Two of soccer's greatest stars in the past 15 years, David Beckham and Cristiano Ronaldo, were handpicked and cultivated by him. They both played in the number 7 shirt, made famous by the likes of George Best, Bryan Robson, and Eric Cantona.

BECKHAM shot to fame when he scored a spectacular goal from the halfway line against Wimbledon on August 17, 1996. His long-range, razor sharp passes were his distinguishing trait, in addition to his lethal free kicks. He was one of United's very best until he transferred to Real Madrid in 2003. He later went to the United States but decided to end his career with Paris Saint-Germain in 2013.

In addition to being a great soccer player, David Beckham is also a huge celebrity. His wife, Victoria, is a successful fashion designer and former pop star, and the two of them frequently grace the gossip columns in magazines.

David Beckham
Born in 1975
With United 1993–2003
394 appearances
85 goals
115 Internationals for England
17 goals

In the summer of 2003 United played a practice match against Sporting in Portugal. An 18-year-old on the Portuguese side impressed United so much that he was almost bought on the spot. Cristiano Ronaldo had a rather slow start with United, he was a bit unreliable to begin with and prone to diving. But he certainly was a diamond in the rough. With time, Ronaldo could do just about anything; he was absurdly skilled, tricky, and a phenomenal scorer. When he transferred to Real Madrid in 2009 it was plain as day that he was one of the best soccer players in history.

Cristiano Ronaldo
Born in 1985
With United 2003–2009
292 appearances
118 goals
105 Internationals for Portugal
40 goals

Hairdryer

When Sir Alex retired as manager of Manchester United in May 2013 he had long been hailed as the most successful manager in the world. He had just won his 13th Premier League title, adding to his silverware of 4 League Cups, 5 FA Cups, 10 FA Charity/Community Shield, and the 2 UEFA Champions League titles, in addition to several other titles and trophies. He had also won the Scottish Premier Division three times and several trophies with Aberdeen. Even though he usually had a good relationship with his players, he was also known for being tough when he deemed necessary. His infamous tirades were called the "hairdryer-treatment" by his players. One such instance, when he was scolding his team at halftime in the locker room, ended with him kicking a soccer boot in frustration that landed on David Beckham's face.

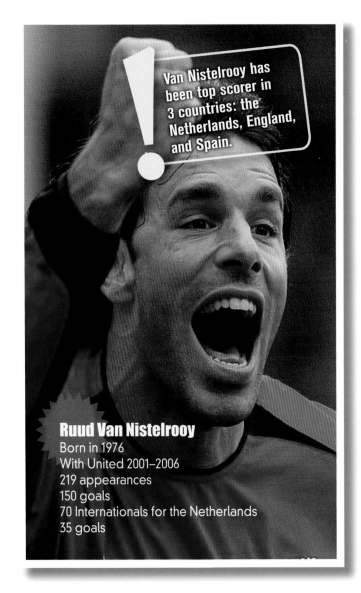

Van Nistelrooy has been top scorer in 3 countries: the Netherlands, England, and Spain.

Both Arsenal and Liverpool had the chance to recruit the young Ronaldo, but felt he was too young. Alex Ferguson saw his potential and did not let the opportunity to sign him pass.

Van Nistelrooy was a natural born scorer. He came to United from PSV Eindhoven in the Netherlands, and had 5 superb seasons as one of the Red Devils. He joined Real Madrid in 2006, like several other United players during that time. It is interesting that of the 150 goals he scored for United only one came from outside the penalty box.

Ruud Van Nistelrooy
Born in 1976
With United 2001–2006
219 appearances
150 goals
70 Internationals for the Netherlands
35 goals

BREAKING ALL RECORDS

Before 1993, Liverpool held more titles and trophies than any other English club. In 1989–90 Liverpool won their 18th First Division title. The following year, Arsenal won their 10th. Everton had claimed the title 9 times, and Aston Villa and Manchester United 7 times each. But then Manchester United started its amazing run that has no equivalent in the English league. In 2010–2011, United broke Liverpool's record by adding its 19th Premiership title to the silverware cabinet. The goal now is to beat Liverpool's English record of five European Champions League titles. United has bagged three so far.

1993	United
1994	United
1995	**Blackburn**
1996	United
1997	United
1998	**Arsenal**
1999	United
2000	United
2001	United
2002	**Arsenal**
2003	United
2004	**Arsenal**
2005	**Chelsea**
2006	**Chelsea**
2007	United
2008	United
2009	United
2010	**Chelsea**
2011	United
2012	**Manchester City**
2013	United

In the 21 seasons of the English Premier League, from 1993–2013, United has won 13 times, while other clubs have won it 8 times all together.

The Youngest Player

David Gaskell, goalkeeper, debuted on October 24, 1956, just 16 years and 19 days old. He played for United the next 13 years, but never became the starting goalkeeper.

David Gaskell

Oldest Player

Billy Meredith

Billy Meredith was almost 47 when he played for United on May 7, 1921. He was one of United's superstars, and famously always played with a toothpick in his mouth. United's oldest player in recent years in Edwin Van der Sar who was

40 years and 211 days old when he appeared in his last match for United on May 28, 2011, against Barcelona.

Ferguson knew he had finally found a worthy replacement for Peter Schmeichel when he took on Van der Sar in 2005. With 130 appearances for the Dutch national team, Van der Sar was the most capped United player, though he only appeared in 24 internationals during his time with United. The most capped player while playing for United was Bobby Charlton with 106 games for England in 1958–70.

Edwin Van der Sar
Born in 1970
With United 2005–2011
266 appearances
Internationals for the Netherlands
130

Most Appearances
in all competitions (as of September 9, 2013)

1.	Ryan Giggs	1991–2013	941
2.	Bobby Charlton	1956–1973	758
3.	Paul Scholes	1994–2013	718
4.	Bill Foulkes	1952–1970	688
5.	Gary Neville	1992–2011	602

Most Goals
in all competitions (as of September 9, 2013)

1.	Bobby Charlton	1956–1973	249
2.	Denis Law	1962–1973	237
3.	Jack Rowley	1937–1955	211
4.	Wayne Rooney	2004–2013	197
5.–6.	George Best	1963–1974	179
5.–6.	Dennis Viollet	1952–1962	179

Most Expensive Players Bought

		When	From	Million £
1.	Berbatov	2008	Tottenham	30.75
2.	Ferdinand	2002	Leeds	29.3
3.	Verón	2001	Lazio	28.1
4.	Rooney	2004	Everton	27.0
5.	Van Persie	2012	Arsenal	24.0

The Most Expensive Players Sold

		When	To	Million £
1.	Ronaldo	2009	R. Madrid	80.0
2.	Beckham	2003	R. Madrid	25.0
3.	Stam	2001	Lazio	15.25
4.	Juan Verón	2003	Chelsea	15.0
5.	Nistelrooy	2006	R. Madrid	10.3
6.	Heinze	2007	R. Madrid	8.1

NEVER GIVE UP

Everyone knows the incredible comeback when United turned around a lost match to win the UEFA Champions League in 1999. That perseverance and will to win installed into the team by Alex Ferguson has brought the club success in many other instances.

Manchester United 3 – Juventus 2

April 21, 1999

Just three weeks prior to the Champions League final in Barcelona, United showed in the semifinals what the team was made of. The Italian giants Juventus had a 2–0 lead after just 11 minutes and Ferguson's hopes of reaching the final seemed to be over. But with great perseverance United managed to score 3 goals in a very tough away game in Turin, and landed a famous victory. United's scorers were Roy Keane, Dwight Yorke, and Andy Cole.

Manchester United 5 – Tottenham 3

September 29, 2001

Tottenham was on top form and at halftime the Spurs were ahead 3–0. But in the first moments of the second half, Andy Cole scored and United took over and simply dominated the match. Laurent Blanc, Van Nistelrooy, and Juan Verón scored one goal after the other, and David Beckham sealed the victory with the final goal in the 87th minute.

The tough-as-nails midfielder, Roy Keane, was a successful captain of United from 1997–2005. He never gave up but he sometimes let his temper get the better of him. All together, he played 480 games for United, with 51 goals.

After 50 minutes Everton had a comfortable 2–0 lead. One of the low-profile but hardworking players Ferguson liked to keep in his team in addition to his stars, John O'Shea, scored in the 61st minute. The second goal came from a former United player, Phil Neville, who made the score. Wayne Rooney and Chris Eagles then secured an unexpected United victory.

Manchester United 5 – Tottenham 2
April 29, 2009

Tottenham once again got to experience the full force of United's fighting spirit. This time the Spurs were again ahead at halftime. In the 56th minute of the match Cristiano Ronaldo scored from a penalty, and in four minutes around the 70th minute he added another and Rooney added two goals. The former Tottenham player, Dimitar Berbatov, then perfected this massive win with a smashing goal in the 79th minute.

Manchester United 4 – West Ham 2
April 2, 2011

West Ham was leading 2–0 at halftime. The club had beaten United 4–0 earlier in the season. Was it possible that they could repeat the feat? Oh, no. Rooney scored a hat trick in 15 minutes in the second half, and Javier Hernández scored United's fourth goal in the final minutes.

Manchester United 3 – Chelsea 3
February 5, 2012

After 50 minutes Chelsea was leading 3–0. Rooney then scored from two penalties and Hernández forced the draw with his goal in the 84th minute of this exciting match.

Unstoppable forwards Dwight Yorke (left) and Andy Cole. Yorke played 147 games 1999–2002, scoring 65 goals. Cole played 275 games in 1995–2001, scoring 121 goals.

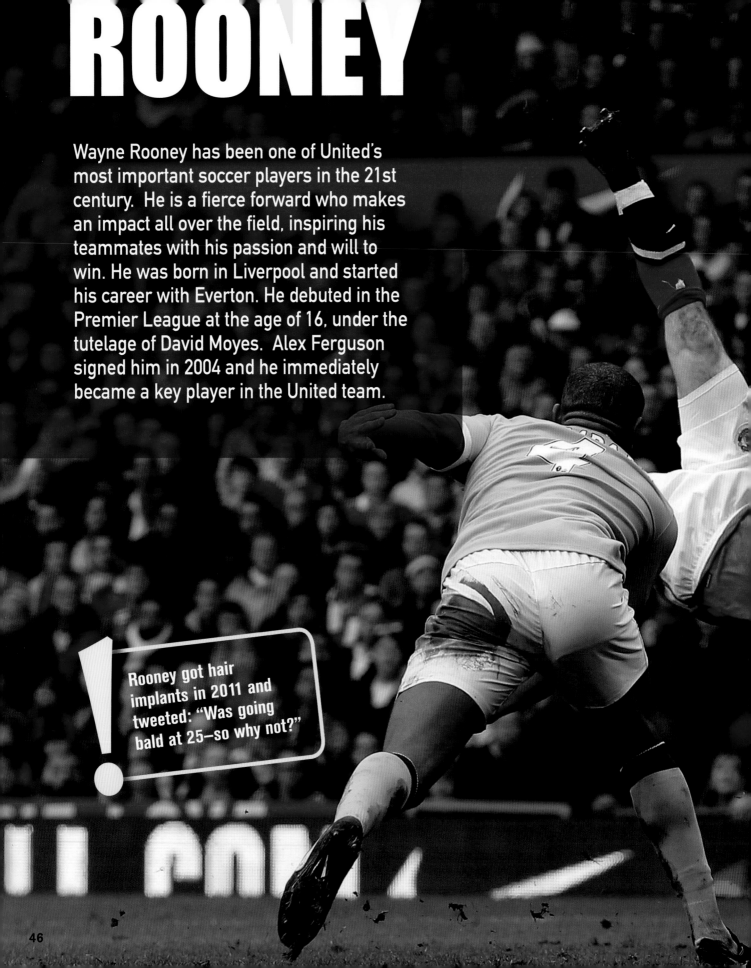

ROONEY

Wayne Rooney has been one of United's most important soccer players in the 21st century. He is a fierce forward who makes an impact all over the field, inspiring his teammates with his passion and will to win. He was born in Liverpool and started his career with Everton. He debuted in the Premier League at the age of 16, under the tutelage of David Moyes. Alex Ferguson signed him in 2004 and he immediately became a key player in the United team.

! Rooney got hair implants in 2011 and tweeted: "Was going bald at 25—so why not?"

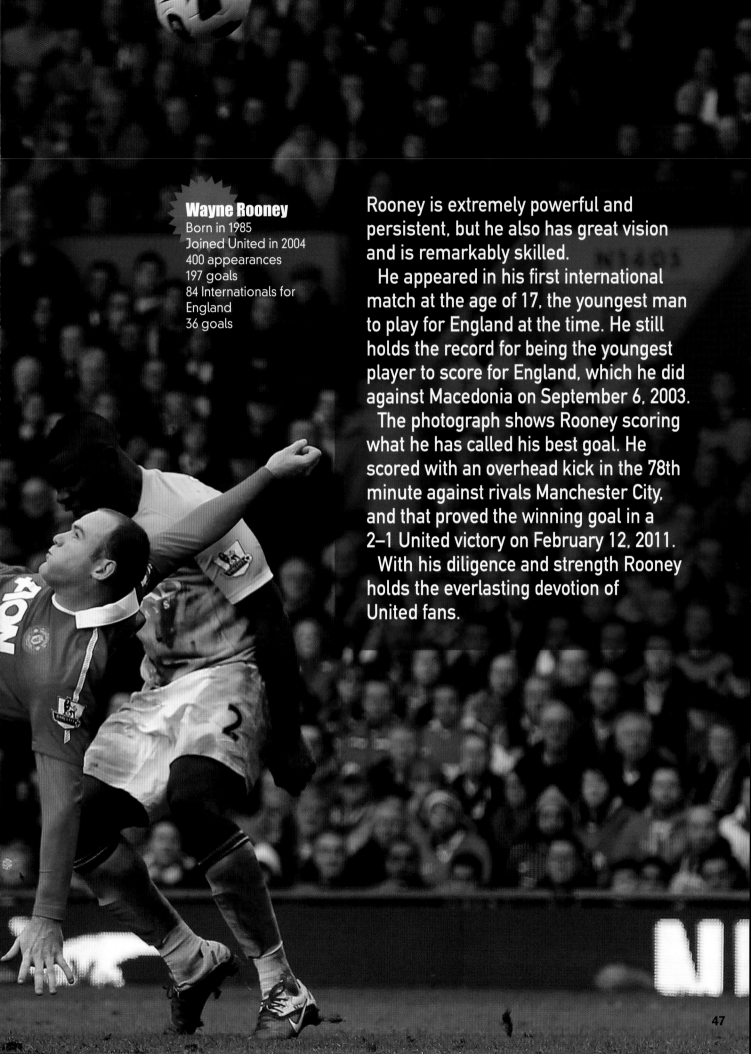

Wayne Rooney
Born in 1985
Joined United in 2004
400 appearances
197 goals
84 Internationals for England
36 goals

Rooney is extremely powerful and persistent, but he also has great vision and is remarkably skilled.

He appeared in his first international match at the age of 17, the youngest man to play for England at the time. He still holds the record for being the youngest player to score for England, which he did against Macedonia on September 6, 2003.

The photograph shows Rooney scoring what he has called his best goal. He scored with an overhead kick in the 78th minute against rivals Manchester City, and that proved the winning goal in a 2–1 United victory on February 12, 2011.

With his diligence and strength Rooney holds the everlasting devotion of United fans.

ROBIN VAN PERSIE

Robin van Persie arrived from Arsenal in the summer of 2012. He scored his first United goal on August 25 against Fulham. During his first season at Old Trafford he scored no less than 30 goals in 48 games. With all due respect to others, van Persie's goals were the main reason Sir Alex Ferguson could celebrate United's 20th league championship title in his last season as manager. Van Persie's second season began magnificently too, when he scored both goals in United's victory over Wigan in the FA Community Shield game. And in the first Premiership game a few days later against Swansea, he also scored two goals. "The Flying Dutchman" just can't stop scoring!

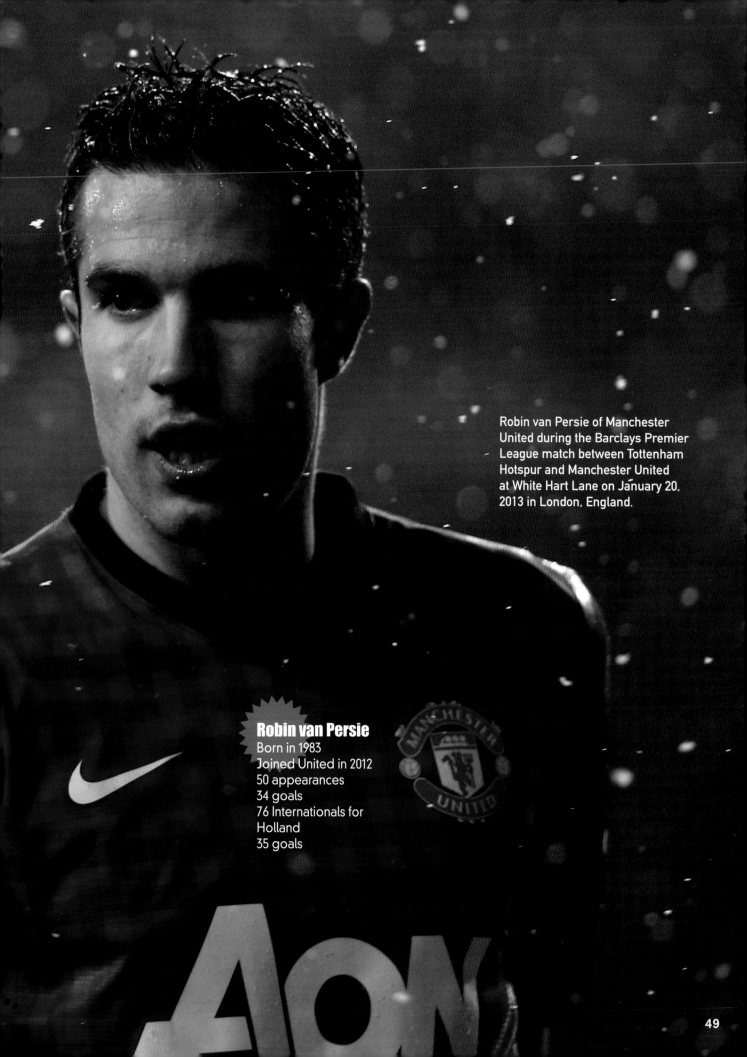

Robin van Persie of Manchester
United during the Barclays Premier
League match between Tottenham
Hotspur and Manchester United
at White Hart Lane on January 20,
2013 in London, England.

Robin van Persie
Born in 1983
Joined United in 2012
50 appearances
34 goals
76 Internationals for
Holland
35 goals

VICTORY IN A MARATHON MATCH

After a long and tough season in the 2007–2008 UEFA Champions League, United made it to the Final in Moscow. United's strikers Rooney, Tévez, and of course Cristiano Ronaldo were a menace to all European clubs, however big. In the semifinals United knocked out the Spanish powerhouse Barcelona, with a winning goal from Scholes at Old Trafford.

The final was against the English club Chelsea. It was an extremely tough match with pouring rain in the second half. Ronaldo was selected Man of the Match by the fans, and he put United in the lead with a goal in the 26th minute, but Frank Lampard scored an equalizer for Chelsea. After extra time the score was still 1–1. John Terry could have won the match for Chelsea in a long and tense penalty shootout, but he missed and United got another chance. The ever-young Ryan Giggs took the last penalty for United and scored. Goalkeeper Van der Saar then denied Nicolas Anelka the equalizing goal for Chelsea. Manchester United was European champion for the third time.

Ryan Giggs set a record when he came on. It was his 759th appearance for United, which meant he broke Bobby Charlton's record for most appearances. In the photo Giggs is celebrating United's third UEFA Champions League title with his teammates.

The Luzhniki Stadium is an artificial turf field but temporary natural grass was installed for the 2008 Champions League Final.

Cristiano Ronaldo had become one of the best soccer players in the world, and was United's best player in the match. He did however fail to score in the penalty shootout.

3

UEFA Champions League

May 21, 2008
Luzhniki Stadium, Moscow, Russia

MAN. UNITED—CHELSEA

7—6

1–1 in regulation time
Ronaldo 26   Lampard 45

Goals from penalties
Tevez, Carrick,   Ballack, Belletti,
Hargreaves, Nani,   Lampard, Cole,
Anderson, Giggs   Kalou

After extra time and penalties.

Van der Sar
Brown (Anderson 120) – Ferdinand – Vidic – Evra
Hargreaves – Scholes (Giggs 87) – Carrick – Ronaldo
Rooney (Nani 101) – Tévez

10 FACTS

Most of the best soccer players of all time play in the World Cup sooner or later. But not all. Two of the strongest soccer players in history who never appeared in the World Cup are United players—George Best from Northern Ireland and Ryan Giggs from Wales. They even played the same position on the left wing.

The Beatles were the most popular band in the world in the mid '60s, and some say they are the best band of all time. The Beatles were from Liverpool, yet in one of their songs they mention Matt Busby, United's manager. The song is called "Dig It" from the album "Let It Be." It is not one of the band's most popular songs, but in it the singer John Lennon lists various things and then he names three famous people—the blues musician B. B. King, singer-actress Doris Day, and finally Busby:

Like a rolling stone
A like a rolling stone
Like the FBI and the CIA
And the BBC, BB King

And Doris Day
Matt Busby
Dig it, dig it, dig it . . .

Ernie Goldthorpe scored the fastest hat trick of any United player. He scored 3 goals in 4 minutes in a match against Notts County 1923. Ole Gunnar Solskjær scored 4 goals in 13 minutes against Nottingham Forest on February 6, 1999.

Manchester United donned jerseys with

SHARP

advertisements on for the first time in 1982. The sponsor was the Japanese electronics company Sharp. United was sponsored by Sharp until 2000, when the club signed a sponsorship contract with Vodafone until 2006. In 2007–2010 United's shirt sponsor was the American AIG insurance, and AON since 2011.

On April 13, 1996, United was down 3–0 at halftime in an away match against Southampton. The team wore a grey away uniform and played badly. The first thing Sir Alex said at halftime was: "Off with the kit!" United appeared in blue and white in the second half and played much better. Southampton still won the game 3–1. United played 5 matches in this drab grey uniform, lost 4 and drew only 1.

Joe Spence was United's best striker from 1919–1933. He started working in the mines at the age of 13, and was conscripted to the army in WWII at the age of 17. He still holds 8th place on the list of United's top scorers, and 9th for most appearances. He played over 510 matches and scored 168 goals. Unbelievably he didn't win a single trophy in all those years with United.

Four clubs have won the English League for 3 consecutive seasons. First Huddersfield 1924–26, then Arsenal 1933–35, and Liverpool 1982–84. Manchester United is the only club to accomplish this *twice*—first in 1999–2001 and then in 2007–2009.

United's first grounds were North Road, and in fact the club was called Newton Heath at the time. North Road had a capacity of 15,000 spectators. From 1893 to 1910 the club played on the Bank Street grounds, which had a capacity of 50,000.

United's players have come from 34 different countries, counting England, Northern Ireland, Scotland, and Wales.

The first player from outside the British Isles or Ireland to play for United was James Brown from 1932 to 1934, who came from the United States. Brown appeared in 41 matches. The next one was another American, Edward McIlvenny who only had two appearances in 1950. But both Brown and McIlvenny were in fact born in Scotland. The third foreigner to join United was the Italian Carlo Sartori in 1968–1973, who had 55 appearances. See also pages 34–35.

UNITED'S CUPS

Manchester United has more top-division titles than any other English club. It has held the First Division/ Premier League title a record 20 times. And the club has also won a host of other titles and trophies. Here is a list of the club's main honors since the first league title in 1908.

FIRST DIVISION / PREMIER LEAGUE
20 times

Most titles:

1.	Manchester United	20
2.	Liverpool	18
3.	Arsenal	13
4.	Everton	9
5.	Aston Villa	7

FA CUP 11 titles

Most FA Cups:

1.	Manchester United	11
2.	Arsenal	10
3.	Tottenham	8
4.–6.	Liverpool	7
	Chelsea	7
	Aston Villa	7

LEAGUE CUP 4 titles
The League Cup was founded in 1961.

Most League Cups:

1.	Liverpool	8
2.	Aston Villa	5
3.–6.	Manchester United	4
	Tottenham	4
	Chelsea	4
	Nottingham Forest	4

United's top-division titles

League titles are awarded for whole seasons. United's first title was awarded for the 1907–1908 season, but for convenience sake only the latter year is listed on this spread. The period between 1913–1947 is left out, as United didn't win any trophies during that time.

	1908	1909	1910	1911	1912	1948	1949	1950	1951	1952	1953	1954	1955	1956	1957	1958	1959	1960	1961	1962	1963	1964	1965	1966	1967	1968	1969	1970	1971	1972	1973	1974	1975
FCWC																																	
ESC																																	
ECWC																																	
EC/ECL																										★							
CS	★			★						★				★	★								★		★								
LC																																	
FAC		★				★															★												
EPL	★			★						★				★	★								★		★								

54

AND TROPHIES

CHARITY/COMMUNITY SHIELD
20 titles

An annual match between the Premier League Champions and holders of the FA Cup.

Most Shields:
1. Manchester United   20
2. Liverpool   15
3. Arsenal   12
4. Everton   9
5. Tottenham   7

UEFA CHAMPIONS LEAGUE
3 titles

Most Champions League Cup/CL wins:
1. Real Madrid, Spain   9
2. AC Milan, Italy   7
3. Liverpool, England   5
4T. Bayern Munich, Germany
     Barcelona, Spain
     Ajax, Holland   4
7.–8. M. United, England   3
      Inter Milan, Italy   3

UEFA CUP WINNERS' CUP
1 title—1991

UEFA SUPER CUP
1 title—1991
An annual match between the winners of the UEFA Champion League and the UEFA Europa League

FIFA CLUB WORLD CUP
2 titles—1999, 2008
Originally a single match between the South American Champions and the European Champions, but since 2000 has been a tournament of champions from 6 continents.

FCWC—FIFA Club World Cup

ESC—UEFA Super Cup

ECWC—UEFA Cup Winners' Cup

EC/ECL—European Cup / UEFA Champions League

CS—Charity/Community Shield

LC—League Cup

FAC—FA Cup

EPL—First Division / Premier League

CURRENT ROSTER

This is the team that David Moyes will be taking over from Sir Alex Ferguson

DAVID DE GEA

Goalkeeper
Spain, born in 1990
Joined 2011
#1

He showed great potential as a goalkeeper early in his career with Atlético Madrid. Ferguson landed him straight into the eye of the storm when Edwin van der Sar retired. At first he did seem a bit nervous and inconsistent, but is getting better all the time.

RAFAEL

Right back
Brazil, born in 1990
Joined 2008
#2

Rafael joined United at a very early age, along with his twin brother Fabio. An attacking and passionate player who has potential to develop further.

RIO FERDINAND

Defender
England, born in 1978
Joined 2002
#5

These are the twilight years of Ferdinand's career. But this intelligent defender has served United well for over 400 matches.

NEMANJA VIDIC

Midfielder
Serbia, born in 1981
Joined 2006
#15

An extremely strong defender who is tough but never rough. Ferguson thought so highly of him that he made him team captain.

PATRICE EVRA

Defender
France, born in 1981
Joined 2006
#3

A lightning fast defender with attacking ambition. He was born in Senegal and had 25 siblings, two of them are deceased.

ANTONIO VALENCIA

Winger
Ecuador, born in 1985
Joined 2009
#25

Skilled and powerful right winger. He scores beautiful goals, even better assists, and can also play right back.

SHINJI KAGAWA

Midfielder
Japan, born in 1989
Joined 2012
#26

A skilled and precise soccer player who Ferguson saw as Scholes' successor in midfield.

MICHAEL CARRICK
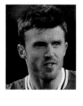

Defensive/central midfielder
England, born in 1981
Joined 2002
#16

Not always the most striking player but he's a hard working midfielder.

JAVIER HERNÁNDEZ "CHICHARITO"

Striker
Mexico, born in 1988
Joined 2010
#14

Agile and diligent, and ready to score at the slightest opportunity. A true poacher in the box.

ROBIN VAN PERSIE

Striker
Netherlands, born in 1983
Joined 2012
#20

Played for Arsenal 2004–2012 and was constantly improving as a soccer player. He scored 132 goals in 277 matches. Joined United to win the titles Arsenal lacked, and brought home the 20th Premier League trophy to Old Trafford. He was the league's top scorer with 26 goals, some of which were pure works of art.

WAYNE ROONEY

Striker
England, born in 1985
Joined 2004
#10

One of the best players in England when he's on top form. See page 46. He is regularly rumored to be heading away from Old Trafford but the fans' loyalty always persuades him to stay! One of the national team's most consistent fighters.

THE BENCH

ANDERS LINDEGAARD
Denmark, born in 1984
—Joined 2010— #13

A powerful and solid goalkeeper, a valuable backup to de Gea, is injured.

JONNY EVANS
Northern Ireland, born in 1988
—Joined 2006—#6

Strong player with great defensive potential.

CHRIS SMALLING
England, born in 1989
—Joined 2010—#12

Strong holding midfielder with great defensive potential.

PHIL JONES
England, born in 1992
—Joined in 2011—#4

A consistent and reliable defender who can also play as a defensive midfielder.

ALEXANDER BUTTNER
Netherlands, born in 1989
—Joined 2012—#28

A promising left back who will be backup to Evra.

RYAN GIGGS
England, born in 1973
—Joined 1990—#11

The evergreen is staying on for one more season!

MAROUANE FELLAINI
Belgium, born 1987
—Joined 2013—#31

A powerful midfielder new manager Moyes knows well from his days of coaching Everton. The only player of note the new manager bought in 2013. Thus has a lot to prove!

ASHLEY YOUNG
England, born in 1985
—Joined 2011—#18

Superbly skilled and tricky left winger with attacking ambition.

TOM CLEVERLEY
England, born in 1989
—Joined 2011—#23

A strong central midfielder.

WILFRIED ZAHA
England, born in 1992
—Joined 2013—#29

An incredibly powerful winger, who could develop into a splendid forward.

ADNAN JANUZAJ
Belgium/Albania, born in 1995
—Joined 2013—#44

A highly promising teenage attacking midfielder.

Heir to the Throne

Even though Alex Ferguson celebrated his 71st birthday on December 31, 2012, it came as a surprise in May 2013 when he announced his retirement as manager. He still seemed to be on top form! But nobody was surprised when he chose David Moyes as his replacement. Moyes had managed Everton for over a decade with fine results. Despite not having the financial capacity of some of the managers of larger clubs, Moyes had been very practical in his management and continually kept Everton in the top half of the Premier League. He was expected to continue with the style of soccer that Sir Alex has had the team play, where solid planning, an attacking front, and a fighting spirit go hand in hand.

Moyes was born in 1963 and is a Scot like Ferguson. He used to be a soccer player himself, playing for clubs in the lower divisions in England before becoming a manager for Preston, and later Everton.

Moyes is always calm on the sidelines.

FAMOUS FANS

License to score?

Sean Connery is a Scottish actor who was the first to portray James Bond in the British film series. He took on Bond's role in seven films from 1962–83, and to many he is the one and only true Bond. In his youth Connery was a talented soccer player and in 1953 he appeared in a practice match watched by Matt Busby, manager of United. Busby was impressed by the passionate Connery and offered him a contract. "I really wanted to accept," Connery later said, "because I loved soccer, but I realized that a top-class soccer player could be over the hill by the age of 30, and I was already 23. I decided to become an actor."

So Connery declined the chance of becoming one of the "Busby Babes," where he would no doubt have had a *license to score*. But Connery has always had a soft spot for United since, and he continued to play soccer for fitness and fun.

Pleading with Sir Alex to play

Usain Bolt from Jamaica is the fastest human being on the planet. He holds the world records in both 100m and 200m sprints. He is also a soccer enthusiast, and has expressed his wish to become a professional soccer player with his favorite club, Manchester United, several times. He pleaded with Ferguson in the media: "I would

Connery

Bolt

of course be the fastest man on the team, but I've also got some other skills." Bolt has been an honorary guest at United matches and visited the training grounds. In 2012 Ferguson claimed he would get a chance in a charity game in 2013. Sadly, this had not yet happened.

Britain's most influential rock bands. He is a passionate United follower, like so many British musicians.

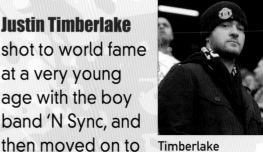

Justin Timberlake shot to world fame at a very young age with the boy band 'N Sync, and then moved on to a very successful solo career and acting. He is from the United States but is a great soccer enthusiast, and his favorite club is Manchester United.

Timberlake

Screen siren Megan Fox became a household name after starring in the first two *Transformers* films, where she showed that she is one tough cookie. She was born in the United States but is a great United fan. She is often photographed wearing the red shirt, even one with a picture of the Mexican prodigy Chicharito on the front.

Fox

The American rapper Snoop Dogg is a great sports fan. He often dons sports jerseys on stage and has worn the Red Devils' shirt on several occasions. He is good friends with former United player, David Beckham.

Many celebrities follow Manchester United!

Thom Yorke is the lead singer and songwriter of Radiohead, one of

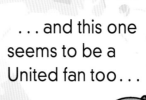

Yorke

. . . and this one seems to be a United fan too . . .

Learn More!

Books

- *The Official Illustrated History of Manchester United 1878–2012: The Full Story and Complete Record*, by Manchester United Football Club and Sir Bobby Charlton
- *Alex Ferguson, My Autobiography*, by Sir Alex Ferguson

Websites

- Manchester United maintains an accessible website in many languages, manutd.com, where you can find everything you would want to know about the club and its history, players, games, and results.
- The **Wikipedia** entry on Manchester United holds an abundance of information about the club.
- espnfc.com (Soccernet)
- goal.com
- 101greatgoals.com
- fourfourtwo.com
- bbc.co.uk/sport/football/teams/manchester-united

Glossary

Striker: A forward player positioned closest to the opposing goal who has the primary role of receiving the ball from teammates and delivering it to the goal.

Winger: The player who keeps to the margins of the field and receives the ball from midfielders or defenders and then sends it forward to the awaiting strikers.

Offensive midfielder: This player is positioned behind the team's forwards and seeks to take the ball through the opposing defense. They either pass to the strikers or attempt a goal themselves. This position is sometimes called "number 10" in reference to the Brazilian genius Pelé, who more or less created this role and wore shirt number 10.

Defensive midfielder: Usually plays in front of his team's defense. The player's central role is to break the offense of the opposing team and deliver the ball to their team's forwards. The contribution of these players is not always obvious but they nevertheless play an important part in the game.

Central midfielder: The role of the central midfielder is divided between offense and defense. The player mainly seeks to secure the center of the field for their team. Box-to-box midfielders are versatile players who possess such strength and foresight that they constantly spring between the penalty areas.

Fullbacks (either left back or right back): Players who defend the sides of the field, near their own goal, but also dash up the field overlapping with wingers in order to lob the ball into the opponent's goal. The fullbacks are sometimes titled wing backs if they are expected to play a bigger role in the offense.

Center backs: These players are the primary defenders of their teams, and are two or three in number depending on formation. The purpose of the center backs is first and foremost to prevent the opponents from scoring and then send the ball towards the center.

Sweeper: The original purpose of the sweeper was to stay behind the defending teammates and "sweep up" the ball if they happened to lose it, but also to take the ball forward. The position of the sweeper has now been replaced by defensive midfielders.

Goalkeeper: Prevents the opponent's goals and is the only player who is allowed to use their hands!

Pick Your Team!

Who do you think should make up the starting eleven at Manchester United? Pick your players — they don't have to be United players, you can pick anyone you think might make sense on the United team. Don't forget to pick your Coach!

Goalkeeper:

Right back:

Left back:

Midfielder:

Midfielder:

Midfielder:

Midfielder:

Right Winger:

Left Winger:

Forward:

Forward:

Coach:

6

5

8

11

Long dry spell. Wait 2 rounds.

Man U w the Europe Cup for the time. What y Go forward many places a last digit in date.

First FA Cup title. Go forward 1 place!

Matt Busby becomes manager. Roll again!

United is the strongest team in England. Jump up and down and then roll again!

You win the First Division title again. Roll again.

Play with one die

The club changes its name to Manchester United. Go forward 4 places.

Players decide whether they must land exactly or not on the last place to win.

Kick off as Newton Heath.

MANCHESTER UNITED

62